THE SEA AND THE BELLS

El mar y las campanas

OTHER BOOKS BY PABLO NERUDA
FROM COPPER CANYON PRESS

Still Another Day
translated by William O'Daly

The Separate Rose
translated by William O'Daly

Winter Garden
translated by William O'Daly

Stones of the Sky
translated by James Nolan

PABLO NERUDA

The Sea and the Bells

TRANSLATED BY WILLIAM O'DALY

COPPER CANYON PRESS : PORT TOWNSEND

Translations from *The Sea and the Bells* have appeared in
American Poetry Review and *Crab Creek Review*.

Publication of this book was made possible by a grant from
the National Endowment for the Arts.

Copper Canyon Press is in residence with Centrum at Fort
Worden State Park.

ISBN 1-55659-018-0 (cloth)
ISBN 1-55659-019-9 (paper)
Library of Congress Catalog Card Number 88-070585

Cover monotype by Galen Garwood.
The type is Sabon, set by Fjord Press Typography.

COPPER CANYON PRESS
Post Office Box 271
Port Townsend
Washington 98368

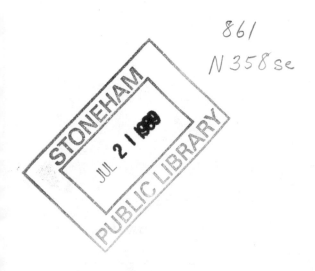

CONTENTS

TRANSLATOR'S ACKNOWLEDGEMENTS

For her keen sense of Pablo Neruda's poems and for her many insightful suggestions, my special thanks to Martha Klindt far south in Venezuela. Stephanie Lutgring read the manuscript and once more offered several clarifications which benefited the translations. My gratitude also goes to John Ellison and to Lesley Link for their editorial skills, for typing the Introduction, and for their encouragement and support. To my Spanish-speaking friends in International who patiently answered my questions and offered strong coffee, I send *un abrazo* and good cheer.

This translation is dedicated to my grandfather,
William C. O'Daly.

INTRODUCTION

Sea salt, foam, the ocean's wave, the sound of bells carrying over the water or striking the Andes, his love for his wife, Matilde, the migratory birds and winter rain of southern Chile, the birth in gunfire of his country, the destiny of the Chilean people – all of these passions helped guide Pablo Neruda's "flight of spirit" as he composed *The Sea and the Bells*. Aware he was dying, Neruda took heightened pleasure in the coastal life surrounding his home in Isla Negra, and he fashioned each day from the past, pulling "one dream out of another."

This is one of eight books of poems he worked on simultaneously (with his memoirs) during his last year of life. He had planned to publish the eight books on his seventieth birthday in July 1974. As it was, Neruda died in September 1973, having given titles to only one-third of the poems in *The Sea and the Bells*. His passions, questions, memories and dreams had carried him like a ship to stand before his image of the "door of earth," a once rugged rock that the waves shape but can never open. This book is preparation by the poet to pass through that door.

In a posthumous book of prose, *Passions and Impressions* (1978), Neruda says that the sacred duty of the poet "is to leave and to return." He must leave his country to encounter other people and places, and he must be aware of the process of spiritual rebirth as one element of the journey. Neruda first experienced travel riding through the Andean foothills in a locomotive with his engineer father, stopping briefly at the small stations where impoverished Araucanian families sold their goods. As a young man, he sailed around much of the world, from consulship to consulship, stopping at ports he probably never imagined as a boy exploring the forests of *La Frontera*. The consular posts he held served as political and spiritual awakenings for Neruda, especially in Barcelona and Madrid (1934–1937). In contrast to his early years in the Orient as a low-level diplomat leading an isolated and frugal life, the Spanish years were filled with camaraderie, artistic exchange, and political solidarity with the Republic, the poets, and with workers' issues. He heard reports of exiled and murdered friends, and he was aware of the devastating effects of the civil war on families and on his own life. He returned to Chile with a fuller understanding of the relationship between political action and people's lives, a poet who was beginning to define his social responsibilities.

His connection to the rain and the forests of his childhood grew stronger every time he left and returned to his country. In the *Memoirs,* Neruda tells the story of going to his father's burial place to move the coffin. As they picked up the coffin, probably cracked by the dampness of the mausoleum, a "torrent of water," rainwater from Chile's southern winter, spilled out of it. For Neruda, the water drove home a reminder as nothing before ever had that he was heir to "an inescapable connection with a predetermined life, region and death." The elements of nature became more and more a connection to the deepest part of himself and a way out of himself, a way of putting the human world in perspective. In the *Residencias* written in the ten years before the Spanish Civil War, Neruda often expressed his internal state in contorted images of the natural world. In *The Sea and the Bells,* he celebrates the regenerative power of nature, specifically elements of southern Chilean landscapes and seascapes, as a primary source of spiritual renewal for him. Speaking of a small river and of himself as a young poet, Neruda recounts his birth of spirit:

> There in the mountain ranges of my country
> at times and long ago
> I saw, touched and heard
> that which was being born:
> a heartbeat, a sound among the stones
> was that which was being born.

As James Nolan says in his introduction to *Stones of the Sky,* "The lesson of stone (for Neruda) is that man is only a tentative stage in the millennial dance of matter toward the crystalline light of the emerald or sapphire or ruby: 'the only star that is ours.' " Matter's inexorable march toward breaking into light is the most intimate form of participation in the day. The purity of nature, of stone and water, of elements that in their basic existence declare what they are, are counterpoints to human beings. If the cyclic processes of nature clarify the processes of our lives, they also declare the truth of our mortality. In *The Sea and the Bells,* our final homecoming is to death and its pure silence:

> Because it is our duty
> to obey winter,
> to let the wind grow
> within you as well,
> until the snow falls,
> until this day and every day are one,
> the wind and the past,
> the cold falls,
> finally we are alone,
> and finally we will be silent.
> Gracias.

Evident in the character of these poems is a new vulnerablity, Neruda's nakedness standing before his readers and the door of earth, having left to him "only the stark noon of the sea and one bell," his voice, with which to offer thanks and to witness his truths.

These poems further develop the theme of the poet reassessing his role as *poeta del pueblo* (poet of the people) that recurs throughout other late books, including *Winter Garden* and *Still Another Day.* In his memoirs, Neruda tells us that "Poetry is a deep inner calling in man; from it came liturgy, the psalms, and also the content of religions. The poet confronted nature's phenomena and in the early ages called himself a priest, to safeguard

3

his vocation. In the same way, to defend his poetry, the poet of the modern age accepts the investiture earned in the street, among the masses. Today's social poet is still a member of the earliest order of priests. In the old days he made his pact with darkness, and now he must interpret the light." While he set himself apart from others in response to his longing later in life for solitude and silence, he reaffirms his own humanity and questions his existence. People attempt to square themselves with their responsibilities during a crisis of the spirit. As *poeta del pueblo,* Neruda wanted to return the gift of his investiture to the Chilean people. The poet asks us to pay close attention as he accounts for his participation in the light:

> With my hands I must
> beckon: somebody please come.
>
> Here is what I have and what I owe,
> please listen to the count, the story, and the sound.
>
> With these things, I pull for every tomorrow of my life
> one dream out of another.

The harsh self-assessment of his performance as a socially committed poet is an important theme in the posthumous books. In *Winter Garden,* Neruda accepts solitude as a faithful companion who will accompany him on his final journey toward clarity. In *The Sea and the Bells,* he longs for the pure silence in which a human being may listen intently and which in death becomes an affirmation of the cyclic power of nature, "the simple truth of a yellow branch."

In this book, Neruda arrived at a new height in his search for a direct and accessible language that would resonate for its clarity. He wanted to write a poetry that would return the gift of his investiture, transformed by a committed life and a generous spirit. Even with their sadness and anger, these poems affirm life, the acceptance of diversity with compassion, and the taking of responsibility for one's own destiny.

While translating *The Sea and the Bells,* it was enlightening and humbling for me to watch this venerable man come to terms with a lifetime of choices, of having acted and not acted, before he died. As he squares himself with his past, Neruda fulfills a requirement for enacting the process of benign cultural and political change in Hispanic America, according to one of the leading inheritors of the poet's role as political commentator. "The rebirth of imagination, in the realm of art as in that of politics, has always been prepared for and preceded by analysis and criticism," writes Octavio Paz in *Convergences.* "I believe that this duty has fallen to our generation and the next. But before undertaking the criticism of our societies, their history and their actuality, we Hispanic American writers must begin by criticizing ourselves. First, we must cure ourselves of the intoxication of simplistic and simplifying ideologies." Neruda does not approach his readers armed with an ideological system and its rhetoric – instead he gives us personal values, clear distinctions, and a celebration of the various forms of love. This may be his most personal book of poems, imbued with deep compassion and vulnerability.

> The world is bluer and of the earth
> at night, when I sleep
> enormous, within your small hands.

Thomas McGrath, another poet who has been shaped in part by Neruda's public commitments and his poetry, describes a passionate and moral life that Neruda would have supported. "I believe that all of us live twice: once personally and once as a representative man or woman. I am interested in those moments when my life line crosses through the concentration points of the history of my time. Then I live both personally and representatively. I hope to be aware of those moments, because then, I believe, one may be speaking to and for many people." Neruda lived as a representative man throughout his life, as a consul, senator, organizer, ambassador, social critic, and poet. The late books suggest he understood the consequences of political action on people's lives, not in a numerical way, but as a fellow citizen, an artist, a husband, and a father. (His only child, Malva Marina, died at age eight in 1942.)

The posthumous books may be thought of as "unfinished," but this label should not obscure our understanding of the poems. *The Sea and the Bells, Winter Garden, The Separate Rose, Stones of the Sky,* and *Still Another Day* form a series of books that are among Neruda's most accessible and profound work. Although they are remarkably different from one another in the orientation of their metaphors and in their voices, they are intimately related by the poet's recurrent passions and by their own symphonic sounds. In these books, Neruda pays tribute to what he identifies in *Passions and Impressions* as "the movement, the surroundings, the unmarked roads, perhaps the inevitability" that caused him to return continually in his life and in his poetry "to these frontiers in the rainswept South, to these great rivers . . . , to the generous silence of these lands and these people." These elements and essences were sources of spiritual renewal for Neruda, like the blue voice of air or the ringing of a bell, that offered him healing by the purity of their existence. Long gone are the moments of special pleading to be heard, the melodic lyricism and the grandeur of *Twenty Love Poems*; and the melancholy of what Paz calls the "mythical geologies" of *Residencias I & II* is no longer pervasive. The late books are marked by the poet's returning to the sources of his pain, anger, wonder, love, and crystallizing them in focused images and modulated tones. These books base their final assessment of the poet's life on political and personal actions, and on his efforts to meet everyone's expectations of him, to speak to and for everybody. In *Winter Garden,* Neruda recounts the difficulty of the task:

6

it was my duty to understand everybody, becoming delirious,
weak, unyielding, compromised, heroic, vile,
loving until I wept, and sometimes an ingrate,
a savior entangled in his own chains,
all dressed in black, toasting to joy.

In the last fourteen books, Neruda's language developed into one perfectly suited to the role of *poeta del pueblo*. Line by line, the lyric quality of *The Sea and the Bells* is not as opulent as in much of Neruda's canon. "This broken bell . . ." is a good example of how the poems rely on expansion and contraction of vowel sounds, and on the heavily cadenced lines to set the basic rhythm for the book. The poems are full of resonance and the rhythm of waves and bells:

El bronce roto y verde,
la campana de bruces
y dormida
fue enredada por las enredaderas,
y del color oro duro del bronce
pasó a color de rana:
fueron las manos del agua,
la humedad de la costa,
que dio verdura al metal,
ternura a la campana.

The bronze cracked and green,
the bell with its mouth open to the ground
and sleeping
was entangled in bindweed,
and the hard golden color of the bronze
turned the color of a frog:
it was the hands of water,
the dampness of the coast
dealt green to the metal
and tenderness to the bell.

Five decades of poetic development produced a poetry of clear and simple images. In "One returns to the self ... ," even the complex need for spiritual rebirth is represented by images of common clothing and houses.

The colloquial language of this book might be called a "public" language, not only for the issues it addresses but for its accessibility. This language is direct and unadorned, and the quiet intensity of its music keeps a dignified tone. Its clarity is meant to incite the recognition of our own truths; its sources are the precise word and silence. In "Pedro is the When ... ," Neruda draws our attention to the piles of words we misuse or use to no purpose every day, the nets of little words we ensnare ourselves in. The public language of *The Sea and the Bells* is intended to challenge the illusions we cast with words, and to act as antidote to the distorted languages of advertising agencies and bureaucracies. In "I met the Mexican ... ," Neruda speaks in a public voice when he reclaims his spiritual ancestry to the people who set a revolution in motion in the Americas when the colonizers arrived, "exchanging coupons for silence." And in "The whole human earth ... ," he draws together in a single constellation the human ability to obscure social memory with economic "progress," the use of misleading language, the revision of history, and the cyclic nature of warfare.

As a balance to the public language of the poems, Neruda developed an understated and sometimes "unspoken" language in this book, especially in the love poems to Matilde. This "private" language is based on sensory awareness between the self and the other, between the poet and the reader – it resonates only when woven into the fabric of the public language. And because its sound exists in and around what the poems explicitly say, the private language is a a communication that encourages intimacy. The relationship between the two languages, these awarenesses, parallels *yin* and *yang*. The private language, *yin,* expresses the intuitive knowledge within the poems, an understanding of silence.

One form of the private language is the unspoken communication between lovers. Referring to Matilde from the southern town of Chillán, he writes:

> she is the one,
> who goes and goes,
> ready for my body,
> for the space of my body,
> opening all the windows to the sea
> so that the written word flies off,
> so that the furniture fills
> with silent signals,
> with green fire.

Perhaps the "silent signals" sent between lovers is a common enough experience that most readers will be able to appreciate the importance of the silent dialogue. The image is all the more sensuous for being left "unspoken," an invitation to the reader to consider his or her own intimate experiences. Neruda's private language often resonates with bells rung in the reader's memory, not only in these ways but in the way it gathers meaning with the repetition of thematic words, cadences, images and sounds.

The sound of bells is an essential part of Neruda's private language, that pure sound with emptiness at its center. It can be initially a public language or a code understood by a community, perhaps to secure the safety of ships near the coast. Ship's bells toll the hour, one hour ending so another can begin. But as the sound travels over the ocean or through the forest, and falls into silence, it becomes private. It's a language we speak to the earth, an invocation, and a sound whose meaning the bellringer himself no longer fully comprehends. The ringing, with a power crystallized in its silence, summons us or turns us around or stops us in our tracks, while the sound waves continue on to strike wild gardens, mountains, and butterflies. It's an element that sounds every day of our lives and at death, and we understand its voice to be truth.

The seamless weave of the two languages in *The Sea and the Bells* is the result of the breadth of Neruda's vision. In these last poems, he strove for and achieved a voice in which a declaration of love for Matilde in the same breath as his love for the earth is a natural articulation. And at the end of his life as a prolific poet and a distinguished public figure, his singular voice asks us to have compassion for ourselves and for others. He reminds us that everything is in process, moving toward the light.

WILLIAM O'DALY
July 4, 1988

THE SEA AND THE BELLS

El mar y las campanas

INICIAL

Hora por hora no es el día,
es dolor por dolor:
el tiempo no se arruga,
no se gasta:
mar, dice el mar,
sin tregua,
tierra, dice la tierra:
el hombre espera.
Y sólo
su campana
allí está entre las otras
guardando en su vacío
un silencio implacable
que se repartirá cuando levante
su lengua de metal ola tras ola.

De tantas cosas que tuve,
andando de rodillas por el mundo,
aquí, desnudo,
no tengo más que el duro mediodía
del mar, y una campana.

Me dan ellos su voz para sufrir
y su advertencia para detenerme.

FIRST MOVEMENT

Hour by hour, the day does not pass,
it passes sadness by sadness:
time does not wrinkle,
it doesn't run out:
sea, the sea says,
without rest,
earth, the earth says:
man waits.
And only
his bell
rings above the others
keeping in its emptiness
the implacable silence
that will be parceled out when
its metallic tongue rises, wave after wave.

Once I had so much,
walking on my knees through the world,
here, naked,
I have nothing more than the stark noon
of the sea, and one bell.

They give me their voice to feel the pain
and their warning to stop me.

Esto sucede para todo el mundo:
continúa el espacio.

Y vive el mar.

Existen las campanas.

This happens to everybody:
space goes on.

The sea lives.

The bells exist.

BUSCAR

Del ditirambo a la raíz del mar
se extiende un nuevo tipo de vacío:
no quiero más, dice la ola,
que no sigan hablando,
que no siga creciendo
la barba del cemento
en la ciudad:
estamos solos,
queremos gritar por fin,
orinar frente al mar,
ver siete pájaros del mismo color,
tres mil gaviotas verdes,
buscar el amor en la arena,
ensuciar los zapatos,
los libros, el sombrero, el pensamiento
hasta encontrarte, nada,
hasta besarte, nada,
hasta cantarte, nada,
nada sin nada, sin hacer
nada, sin terminar
lo verdadero.

TO SEARCH

From the dithyramb to the root of the sea
stretches a new kind of emptiness:
I don't want much, the wave says,
only for them to stop their chatter,
for the city's cement beard
to stop growing:
we are alone,
we want at last to scream,
to pee facing the ocean,
to see seven birds of the same color,
three thousand green gulls,
to seek out love on the sand,
to break in our shoes, to dirty
our books, our hat, our mind
until we find you, nothing,
until we kiss you, nothing,
until we sing you, nothing,
nothing without nothing, without being
nothing, without putting an end
to truth.

REGRESANDO

Yo tengo tantas muertes de perfil
que por eso no muero,
soy incapaz de hacerlo,
me buscan y no me hallan
y salgo con la mía,
con mi pobre destino
de caballo perdido
en los potreros solos
del sur del Sur de América:
sopla un viento de fierro,
los árboles se agachan
desde su nacimiento:
deben besar la tierra,
la llanura:
llega después la nieve
hecha de mil espadas
que no terminan nunca.
Yo he regresado
desde donde estaré,
desde mañana Viernes,
yo regresé
con todas mis campanas
y me quedé plantado
buscando la pradera,
besando tierra amarga
como el arbusto agachado.

RETURNING

So many profiles of death line my face
that I cannot die,
I'm not capable of it,
they look for me and can't find me
and I leave with what is mine,
with my poor destiny
on horseback, lost
in solitary pastures
far south in South America:
a fiery wind blows in,
the trees are bent down
from the day of their birth:
they must kiss the earth,
that smooth plain:
it comes later, the snow
of a thousand swords
that never lets up.
I have returned
from where I will go,
on Friday tomorrow
I came back
with each of my bells
and I stood waiting,
searching for the meadow,
kissing bitter earth
like a bent-over shrub.

Porque es obligatorio
obedecer al invierno,
dejar crecer el viento
también dentro de ti,
hasta que cae la nieve,
se unen el hoy y el día,
el viento y el pasado,
cae el frío,
al fin estamos solos,
por fin nos callaremos.
Gracias.

Because it is our duty
to obey winter,
to let the wind grow
within you as well,
until the snow falls,
until this day and every day are one,
the wind and the past,
the cold falls,
finally we are alone,
and finally we will be silent.
Gracias.

Gracias, violines, por este día
de cuatro cuerdas. Puro
es el sonido del cielo,
la voz azul del aire.

I am grateful, violins, for this day
of four chords. Pure
is the sound of the sky,
the blue voice of air.

Parece que un navío diferente
pasará por el mar, a cierta hora.
No es de hierro ni son anaranjadas
sus banderas:
nadie sabe de dónde
ni la hora:
todo está preparado
y no hay mejor salón, todo dispuesto
al acontecimiento pasajero.
Está la espuma dispuesta
como una alfombra fina,
tejida con estrellas,
más lejos el azul,
el verde, el movimiento ultramarino,
todo espera.
Y abierto el roquerío,
lavado, limpio, eterno,
se dispuso en la arena
como un cordón de castillos,
como un cordón de torres.
Todo
está dispuesto,
está invitado el silencio,
y hasta los hombres, siempre distraídos,
esperan no perder esta presencia:
se vistieron como en día Domingo,
se lustraron las botas,
se peinaron.
Se están haciendo viejos
y no pasa el navío.

_____

It appears that a different ship
will sail across the sea, at a certain hour.
She isn't built of iron and does not fly
orange flags:
nobody knows from where
or the hour:
everything is arranged
and there is no finer salon, everything is ready
for the fleeting event.
The spume is rolled out
like an elegant carpet
woven with stars,
the blue even farther,
the greenness, the movement from another sea,
everything waits.
And the scattered rookery,
washed, gleaming, eternal,
lined itself up across the sand
like a chain of castles,
like a chain of towers.
Everything
is prepared,
silence is invited,
and even men, always distracted,
hope not to miss this apparition:
they are dressed in Sunday suits,
their boots are shined,
their hair combed.
They are growing older
and the ship does not sail.

_____

Cuando yo decidí quedarme claro
y buscar mano a mano la desdicha
para jugar a los dados,
encontré la mujer que me acompaña
a troche y moche y noche,
a nube y a silencio.

Matilde es ésta,
ésta se llama así
desde Chillán,
y llueva
o truene o salga
el día con su pelo azul
o la noche delgada,
ella,
déle que déle,
lista para mi piel,
para mi espacio,
abriendo todas las ventanas del mar
para que vuele la palabra escrita,
para que se llenen los muebles
de signos silenciosos,
de fuego verde.

When I decided to clarify my life
and, hand by hand, to seek out misfortune
by throwing the dice,
I met the woman who accompanies me
everywhere and at all hours,
in clouds and in silence.

Matilde is the one
who answers to this name
from Chillán,
and even if it rains
or thunders or rises,
the day with blue hair
or the slender night,
she is the one,
who goes and goes,
ready for my body,
for the space of my body,
opening all the windows to the sea
so that the written word flies off,
so that the furniture fills
with silent signals,
with green fire.

Declaro cuatro perros:
uno ya está enterrado en el jardín,
otros dos me sorprenden,
minúsculos salvajes
destructores,
de patas gruesas y colmillos duros
como agujas de roca.
Y una perra greñuda,
distante,
rubia en su cortesía.
No se sienten sus pasos de oro suave,
ni su distante presencia.
Sólo ladra muy tarde por la noche
para ciertos fantasmas,
para que sólo ciertos ausentes escogidos
la oigan en los caminos
o en otros sitios oscuros.

———————

I have four dogs to declare:
one is already buried in the garden,
two others keep me on my toes,
tiny wild
destroyers,
with thick paws and hard canines
like needles of stone.
And one scruffy dog,
aloof,
fair-haired in her gracious manner.
No one hears her smooth golden steps
or her distant presence.
She barks only late at night
at certain phantoms,
so that just a few chosen hidden persons
hear her on the roads
or in other dark places.

Vinieron unos argentinos,
eran de Jujuy y Mendoza,
un ingeniero, un médico,
tres hijas como tres uvas.
Yo no tenía nada que decir.
Tampoco mis desconocidos.
Entonces no nos dijimos nada,
sólo respiramos juntos
el aire brusco del Pacífico sur,
el aire verde
de la pampa líquida.
Tal vez se lo llevaron de vuelta a sus ciudades
como quien se lleva un perro de otro país,
o unas alas extrañas,
un ave palpitante.

Some Argentinians sailed with us,
they were from Jujuy and Mendoza,
an engineer, a doctor,
three daughters like three grapes.
I had nothing to say.
Nor did the strangers.
So nobody said a word,
but together we inhaled
the crisp air of the South Pacific,
the green air
of the liquid pampa.
Maybe they carried it back to their cities
as one returns with a dog from another country,
or a bird with strange wings,
a fluttering bird.

Yo me llamaba Reyes, Catrileo,
Arellano, Rodríguez, he olvidado
mis nombres verdaderos.
Nací con apellido
de robles viejos, de árboles recientes,
de madera silbante.
Yo fui depositado
en la hojarasca:
se hundió el recién nacido
en la derrota y en el nacimiento
de selvas que caían
y casas pobres que recién lloraban.
Yo no nací sino que me fundaron:
me pusieron todos los nombres a la vez,
todos los apellidos:
me llamé matorral, luego ciruelo,
alerce y luego trigo,
por eso soy tanto y tan poco,
tan multitud y tan desamparado,
porque vengo de abajo,
de la tierra.

My name was Reyes, Catrileo,
Arellano, Rodríguez, I have forgotten
my true names.
I was born with a surname
of old oaks, of saplings,
of hissing wood.
I was deposited
among rotting leaves:
this newborn sank down
in the defeat and in the birth
of forests that were falling
and poor houses that had recently been weeping.
I was not born but rather they founded me:
all at once they gave me every name,
every family's name:
I was called thicket, then plum tree,
larch and then wheat,
that is why I am so much and so little,
so wealthy and so destitute,
because I come from below,
from the earth.

Salud, decimos cada día,
a cada uno,
es la tarjeta de visita
de la falsa bondad
y de la verdadera.
Es la campana para reconocernos:
aquí estamos, salud!
Se oye bien, existimos.
Salud, salud, salud,
a éste y al otro, a quién,
y al cuchillo, al veneno
y al malvado.
Salud, reconocedme,
somos iguales y no nos queremos,
nos amamos y somos desiguales,
cada uno con cuchara,
con un lamento especial,
encantado de ser o de no ser:
hay que disponer de tantas manos,
de tantos labios para sonreír,
salud!
que ya no queda tiempo.
Salud
de enterarse de nada.
Salud
de dedicarnos a nosotros mismos
si es que nos queda algo de nosotros,
de nosotros mismos.
Salud!

Salud, we called out every day,
to every single person,
it is the calling card
of false kindness
and of sincerity.
It's the bell we are known by:
here we are, salud!
You hear it clearly, we exist.
Salud, salud, salud,
to this one and that one
and the other one,
to the poisoned knife
and to the assassin.
Salud, recognize me,
we are equal and do not like each other,
we love each other and are not equal,
each of us with a spoon,
with our own sad story,
haunted by being and not being:
we all need to have so many hands,
and so many lips to smile,
salud!
time has already passed.
Salud
to getting to know nothing.
Salud
to devoting ourselves to ourselves,
if anything remains of us,
of ourselves.
Salud!

Hoy cuántas horas van cayendo
en el pozo, en la red, en el tiempo:
son lentas pero no se dieron tregua,
siguen cayendo, uniéndose
primero como peces,
luego como pedradas o botellas.
Allá abajo se entienden
las horas con los días,
con los meses,
con borrosos recuerdos,
noches deshabitadas,
ropas, mujeres, trenes y provincias,
el tiempo se acumula
y cada hora
se disuelve en silencio,
de desmenuza y cae
al ácido de todos los vestigios,
al agua negra
de la noche inversa.

Today, how many hours are falling
into the well, into the net, into time:
they go slowly but never stopped to rest,
they keep on falling, swarming together
at first like fish,
then like falling bottles or stones.
There below the hours come
to agree with the days,
with the months,
with blurred memories,
with uninhabited nights,
clothes, women, trains, provinces,
and time collects,
hour upon hour
dissolves in silence,
crumbles and falls
into the acid of all ruins,
into the black water
of the inverted night.

Conocí al mexicano Tihuatín
hace ya algunos siglos, en Jalapa,
y luego de encontrarlo cada vez
en Colombia, en Iquique, en Arequipa,
comencé a sospechar de su existencia.
Extraño su sombrero
me había parecido cuando
el hombre aquel, alfarero de oficio,
vivía de la arcilla mexicana
y luego fue arquitecto, mayordomo
de una ferretería en Venezuela,
minero y alguacil en Guatemala.
Yo pensé cómo, con la misma edad,
sólo trescientos años,
yo, con el mismo oficio, ensimismado
en mi campanería,
con golpear siempre piedras o metales
para que alguien oiga mis campanas
y conozca mi voz, mi única voz,
este hombre, desde muertos años
por ríos que no existen,
cambiaba de ejercicio?

Entonces comprendí que él era yo,
que éramos un sobreviviente más
entre otros de por acá o aquí,
otros de iguales linajes enterrados
con las manos sucias de arena,
naciendo siempre y en cualquiera parte
dispuestos a un trabajo interminable.

I met the Mexican Tihuatín
a few centuries ago, in Jalapa,
and later after each time I found him
in Colombia, in Iquique, in Arequipa,
I began to wonder if he really existed.
His hat had seemed
strange to me when
that man, a potter by trade,
lived by Mexican clay,
later he was an architect, a foreman
in a foundry in Venezuela,
a miner and a governor in Guatemala.
I wondered how, being the same age,
only three hundred years old,
I, of the same trade, daydreaming
in my foundry of bells,
always striking stone or metal
so that someone will hear the sound
and know my voice, my singular voice,
this man, from wasted years
sailing rivers that do not exist,
how was he changed by those changes?

Then I understood that I was he,
that we were one more survivor
among others from here and there,
and those of the same lineage, equal, buried,
their hands crusted with sand,
always being born and everywhere
seized by an endless task.

A ver, llamé a mi tribu y dije: a ver,
quiénes somos, qué hacemos, qué pensamos.
El más pálido de ellos, de nosotros,
me respondió con otros ojos,
con otra sinrazón, con su bandera.
Ese era el pabellón del enemigo.
Aquel hombre, tal vez, tenía derecho
a matar mi verdad, así pasó
conmigo y con mi padre, y así pasa.
Pero sufrí como si me mordieran.

To find out, I called together my tribe and said: let's see
who we are, what we do, what we think.
The whitest of them, of us,
answered me with defiant eyes,
with his separate faith, with his flag.
He was the enemy's fortress.
Perhaps that man had the right
to murder my truth, so it happened
with me and with my father, and so it goes.
But I suffered as if they had sunk their teeth into me.

CADA DIA MATILDE

Hoy a ti: larga eres
como el cuerpo de Chile, y delicada
como una flor de anís,
y en cada rama guardas testimonio
de nuestras indelebles primaveras:
Qué día es hoy? Tu día.
Y mañana es ayer, no ha sucedido,
no se fue ningún día de tus manos:
guardas el sol, la tierra, las violetas
en tu pequeña sombra cuando duermes.
Y así cada mañana
me regalas la vida.

EVERY DAY, MATILDE

Today, I dedicate this to you: you are long
like the body of Chile, delicate
like an anise flower,
and in every branch you bear witness
to our indelible springtimes:
What day is today? Your day.
And tomorrow is yesterday, it has not passed,
the day never slipped from your hands:
you guard the sun, the earth, the violets
in your slender shadow when you sleep.
And in this way, every morning
you give me life.

Les contaré que en la ciudad viví
en cierta calle con nombre de capitán,
y esa calle tenía muchedumbre,
zapaterías, ventas de licores,
almacenes repletos de rubíes.
No se podía ir o venir,
había tantas gentes
comiendo o escupiendo o respirando,
comprando y vendiendo trajes.
Todo me pareció brillante,
todo estaba encendido
y era todo sonoro
como para cegar o ensordecer.
Hace ya tiempo de esta calle,
hace ya tiempo que no escucho nada,
cambié de estilo, vivo entre las piedras
y el movimiento del agua.
Aquella calle tal vez se murió
de muertes naturales.

I will tell you that I lived in a city
on a certain street called Capitán,
that street was jammed with people,
shoe shops, liquor stores,
department stores filled with rubies.
You were not able to come or go,
everywhere there were people
eating or spitting or breathing,
buying and selling clothes.
It all seemed to glitter,
everything was glowing
and everything resounded,
enough to blind or deafen.
A long time has passed since this street,
it's been a long time since I've heard anything,
I changed my life, I live among stones
and the movement of water.
Maybe that street died
a natural death.

De un viaje vuelvo al mismo punto,
por qué?
Por qué no vuelvo donde antes viví,
calles, países, continentes, islas,
donde tuve y estuve?
Por qué será este sitio la frontera
que me eligió, qué tiene este recinto
sino un látigo de aire vertical
sobre mi rostro, y unas flores negras
que el largo invierno muerde y despedaza?
Ay, que me señalan: éste es
el perezoso, el señor oxidado,
de aquí no se movió,
de este duro recinto:
se fue quedando inmóvil
hasta que ya se endurecieron sus ojos
y le creció una yedra en la mirada.

———————

From my journeys I return to the same spot,
why?
Why do I never return to where I used to live,
streets, countries, continents, islands,
where I had something and was?
Why was it the Frontier
that elected me, what does this place have
except a whip of vertical air
above my face, and a few black flowers
that the long winter bites and rips to pieces?
Oh, what are they trying to tell me: we have here
the lazy one, the arthritic gentleman,
from here he never went anywhere,
he stayed in this rough place:
he became immobile
until his eyes hardened
and ivy grew in his stare.

Se vuelve a yo como a una casa vieja
con clavos y ranuras, es así
que uno mismo cansado de uno mismo,
como de un traje lleno de agujeros,
trata de andar desnudo porque llueve,
quiere el hombre mojarse en agua pura,
en viento elemental, y no consigue
sino volver al pozo de sí mismo,
a la minúscula preocupación
de si existió, de si supo expresar
o pagar o deber o descubrir,
como si yo fuera tan importante
que tenga que aceptarme o no aceptarme
la tierra con su nombre vegetal,
en su teatro de paredes negras.

One returns to the self as if to an old house
with nails and slots, so that
a person tired of himself
as of a suit full of holes,
tries to walk naked in the rain,
wants to drench himself in pure water,
in elemental wind, and he cannot
but return to the well of himself,
to the least worry
over whether he existed, whether he knew how to speak his mind
or to pay or to owe or to discover,
as if I were so important
that it must accept or not accept me,
the earth with its leafy name,
in its theater of black walls.

Hace tiempo, en un viaje
descubrí un río:
era apenas un niño, un perro, un pájaro,
aquel río naciente.
Susurraba y gemía
entre las piedras
de la ferruginosa cordillera:
imploraba existencia
entre la soledad de cielo y nieve,
allá lejos, arriba.
Yo me sentí cansado
como un caballo viejo
junto a la criatura natural
que comenzaba a correr,
a saltar y crecer,
a cantar con voz clara,
a conocer la tierra,
las piedras, el transcurso,
a caminar noche y día,
a convertirse en trueno,
hasta llegar a ser vertiginoso,
hasta llegar a la tranquilidad,
hasta ser ancho y regalar el agua,
hasta ser patriarcal y navegado,
este pequeño río,
pequeño y torpe como un pez metálico
aquí dejando escamas al pasar,
gotas de plata agredida,

Long ago, on a journey
I discovered a river:
it was scarcely a child, a dog, a bird,
that newly born river.
It was gurgling and moaning
among the stones
of the iron-stained sierra:
it was begging for life
between the solitudes of sky and snow,
in the distance, high up.
I was as weary
as an old horse
next to the wild creature
that was beginning to run,
to jump and to grow,
to sing with a clear voice,
to know the earth,
stones, passing time,
to travel night and day,
to become thunder,
until getting dizzy,
until entering the calm,
until growing wide and bringing water,
until becoming patriarchal and sailed upon,
this small river,
small and clumsy as a metallic fish
shedding scales as it passes,
drops of assaulted silver,

un río
que lloraba al nacer,
que iba creciendo
ante mis ojos.
Allí en las cordilleras de mi patria
alguna vez y hace tiempo
yo vi, toqué y oí
lo que nacía:
un latido, un sonido entre las piedras
era lo que nacía.

a river
crying to be born,
growing before my eyes.
There in the mountain ranges of my country
at times and long ago
I saw, touched and heard
that which was being born:
a heartbeat, a sound among the stones
was that which was being born.

———————————

Pedro es el cuándo y el cómo,
Clara es tal vez el sin duda,
Roberto, el sin embargo:
todos caminan con preposiciones,
adverbios, sustantivos
que se anticipan en los almacenes,
en las corporaciones, en la calle,
y me pesa cada hombre con su peso,
con su palabra relacionadora
como un sombrero viejo:
a dónde van? me pregunto.
A dónde vamos
con la mercadería
precautoria,
envolviéndonos en palabritas,
vistiéndonos con redes?

A través de nosotros cae como la lluvia
la verdad, la esperada solución:
vienen y van las calles
llenas de pormenores:
ya podemos colgar como tapices
del salón, del balcón, por las paredes,
los discursos caídos
al camino
sin que nadie se quedara con nada,
oro o azúcar, seres verdaderos,
la dicha,
todo esto no se habla,
no se toca,

Pedro is the When and the How,
Clara might say Of Course,
Roberto means Nevertheless:
they all walk with the help of prepositions,
adverbs, nouns
that pile up in the stores,
in the corporations, in the street,
and the weight of each man weighs on me,
on his connecting word
like an old hat:
where are they going? I ask myself.
Where are we going
with merchandise
we chose so carefully,
wrapped in little words,
dressed up in nets of words?

Over us the truth falls
like rain, the long-awaited answer:
the streets come and go
full of particulars:
now we are able to hang, like tapestries
in the drawing room, from the balcony, against the walls,
the speeches that fell
onto the sidewalk
without anyone being left with anything,
gold or sugar, honest lives,
happiness,
all this unspoken,
untouched,

no existe, así parece, nada claro,
piedra, madera dura,
base o elevación de la materia,
de la materia feliz,
nada, no hay sino seres sin objeto,
palabras sin destino
que no van más allá de tú y yo,
ni más acá de la oficina:
estamos demasiado ocupados:
nos llaman por teléfono
con urgencia
para notificarnos que queda prohibido
ser felices.

it seems nothing certain exists,
stone, hard wood,
base or height of matter,
of happy matter,
nothing, there are only beings without purpose,
words without destination,
spoken just between you and me,
that never leave the office:
we are too busy:
they telephone us
with urgent voices
to tell us that it is forbidden
to be happy.

Un animal pequeño,
cerdo, pájaro o perro
desvalido,
hirsuto entre plumas o pelo,
oí toda la noche,
afiebrado, gimiendo.

Era una noche extensa
y en Isla Negra, el mar,
todos sus truenos, su ferretería,
sus toneles de sal, sus vidrios rotos
contra la roca inmóvil, sacudía.

El silencio era abierto y agresivo
después de cada golpe o catarata.

Mi sueño se cosía
como hilando la noche interrumpida
y entonces el pequeño ser peludo,
oso pequeño o niño enfermo,
sufría asfixia o fiebre,
pequeña hoguera de dolor, gemido
contra la noche inmensa del océano,
contra la torre negra del silencio,
un animal herido,
pequeñito,
apenas susurrante
bajo el vacío de la noche,
solo.

A small animal,
pig, bird or dog,
defenseless,
gristled with feathers or fur,
I heard it all night,
fevered, howling.

It was a vast night
and in Isla Negra, the sea,
all of its thunder, its floating hardware,
its tons of salt, its glass broken
against the immobile rock,
the sea shuddered.

The silence was clear and fierce
after every bolt or shower.

My sleep was stitched
by the spinning of the interrupted night
and then the small, shaggy being,
small bear or sick child,
suffered asphyxia or fever,
little bonfire of sadness, a cry
against the immense night of the ocean,
against the black tower of silence,
wounded animal,
so small,
barely whispering
beneath the emptiness of night,
alone.

No hay mucho que contar,
para mañana
cuando ya baje
al Buenosdías
es necesario para mí
este pan
de los cuentos,
de los cantos.
Antes del alba, despés de la cortina
también, abierta al sol del frío,
la eficacia de un día turbulento.

Debo decir: aquí estoy,
esto no me pasó y esto sucede:
mientras tanto las algas del océano
se mecen predispuestas
a la ola,
y cada cosa tiene su razón:
sobre cada razón un movimiento
como de ave marina que despega
de piedra o agua o alga flotadora.

Yo con mis manos debo
llamar: venga cualquiera.

Aquí está lo que tengo, lo que debo,
oigan la cuenta, el cuento y el sonido.

Así cada mañana de mi vida
traigo del sueño otro sueño.

There isn't much to tell,
tomorrow
when I go down
to Goodmorning and How are you
what I really need
is this bread
of the stories,
of the songs.
Before dawn, and after curtains
open to the sun risen from the cold,
the orderly forces of a turbulent day.

I can only say: I am here,
no, that didn't happen and this happens:
meanwhile the ocean's algae constantly
rises and falls, tuned
to the wave,
and everything has its reason:
across every reason a movement
like a seabird that takes flight
from stone or water or floating seaweed.

With my hands I must
beckon: somebody please come.
Here is what I have and what I owe,
please listen to the count, the story, and the sound.

With these things, I pull for every tomorrow of my life
one dream out of another.

Llueve
sobre la arena, sobre el techo
el tema
de la lluvia:
las largas eles de la lluvia lenta
caen sobre las páginas
de mi amor sempiterno,
la sal de cada día:
regresa lluvia a tu nido anterior,
vuelve con tus agujas al pasado:
hoy quiero el espacio blanco,
el tiempo de papel para una rama
de rosal verde y de rosas doradas:
algo de la infinita primavera
que hoy esperaba, con el cielo abierto
y el papel esperaba,
cuando volvió la lluvia
a tocar tristemente
la ventana,
luego a bailar con furia desmedida
sobre mi corazón y sobre el techo,
reclamando
su sitio,
pidiéndome una copa
para llenarla una vez más de agujas,
de tiempo transparente,
de lágrimas.

It rains
over the sand, over the roof
the theme
of the rain:
the long Ls of rain fall slowly
over the pages
of my everlasting love,
this salt of every day:
rain, return to your old nest,
return with your needles to the past:
today I long for the whitest space,
winter's whiteness for a branch
of green rosebush and golden roses:
something of infinite spring
that today was waiting, under a cloudless sky
and whiteness was waiting,
when the rain returned
to sadly drum
against the window,
then to dance with unmeasured fury
over my heart and over the roof,
reclaiming
its place,
asking me for a cup
to fill once more with needles,
with transparent time,
with tears.

En pleno mes de Junio
me sucedió una mujer,
más bien una naranja.
Está confuso el panorama:
tocaron a la puerta:
era una ráfaga,
un látigo de luz,
una tortuga ultravioleta,
la vi
con lentitud de telescopio,
como si lejos fuera o habitara
esta vestidura de estrella,
y por error del astrónomo
hubiera entrado en mi casa.

In fullest June
a woman entered my life,
no, it was an orange.
The scene is blurred:
they knocked on the door:
it was a gust of wind,
a whiplash of light,
an ultraviolet tortoise,
I focused on it
with the slowness of a telescope,
as if it were far away or once inhabited
this vestment of stars,
and by an error of astronomy
had entered my house.

Esta campana rota
quiere sin embargo cantar:
el metal ahora es verde,
color de selva tiene la campana,
color de agua de estanques en el bosque,
color del día en las hojas.

El bronce roto y verde,
la campana de bruces
y dormida
fue enredada por las enredaderas,
y del color oro duro del bronce
pasó a color de rana:
fueron las manos del agua,
la humedad de la costa,
que dio verdura al metal,
ternura a la campana.

Esta campana rota
arrastrada en el brusco matorral
de mi jardín salvaje,
campana verde, herida,
hunde sus cicatrices en la hierba:
no llama a nadie más, no se congrega
junto a su copa verde
más que una mariposa que palpita
sobre el metal caído y vuela huyendo
con alas amarillas.

This broken bell
still wants to sing:
the metal now is green,
the color of woods, this bell,
color of water in stone pools in the forest,
color of day in the leaves.

The bronze cracked and green,
the bell with its mouth open to the ground
and sleeping
was entangled in bindweed,
and the hard golden color of the bronze
turned the color of a frog:
it was the hands of water,
the dampness of the coast,
dealt green to the metal
and tenderness to the bell.

This broken bell
miserable in the rude thicket
of my wild garden,
green bell, wounded,
its scars immersed in the grass:
it calls to no one anymore, no one gathers
around its green goblet
except one butterfly that flutters
over the fallen metal and flies off, escaping
on yellow wings.

Quiero saber si usted viene conmigo
a no andar y no hablar, quiero
saber si al fin alcanzaremos
la incomunicación: por fin
ir con alguien a ver el aire puro,
la luz listada del mar de cada día
o un objeto terrestre
y no tener nada que intercambiar
por fin, no introducir mercaderías
como lo hacían los colonizadores
cambiando barajitas por silencio.
Pago yo aquí por tu silencio.
De acuerdo: yo te doy el mío
con una condición: no comprendernos.

I want to know if you come with me
toward not walking and not speaking, I want
to know if we finally will reach
no communication: finally
going with someone to see pure air,
rays of light over the daily sea
or a landbound object
and finally having nothing
to trade, without goods to furnish
as the colonizers had,
exchanging coupons for silence.
Here I purchase your silence.
I agree: I give you mine
with one provision: that we not understand each other.

(H.V.)

Me sucedió con el fulano aquél
recomendado, apenas conocido,
pasajero en el barco, el mismo barco
en que viajé fatigado de rostros.
Quise no verlo, fue imposible.
Me impuse otro deber contra mi vida:
ser amistoso en vez de indiferente
a causa de su rápida mujer,
alta y bella, con frutos y con ojos.
Ahora veo mi equivocación
en su triste relato de viajero.

Fui generoso provincianamente.

No creció su mezquina condición
por mi mano de amigo, en aquel barco,
su desconfianza en sí siguió más fuerte
como si alguien pudiera convencer
a los que no creyeron en sí mismos
que no se menoscaben en su guerra
contra la propia sombra. Así nacieron.

(H.V.)

It happened to me with some fellow who came
with references, I was getting to know him,
a passenger on the ship, the same ship
on which I was sailing, weary of faces.
I wanted to avoid him – it was impossible.
So, I set myself to do the right thing:
I would be friendly rather than aloof
yet only because of his hot-blooded woman,
tall and beautiful, blooming, and her eyes!
Now, in this traveler's sad tale
I see what I did wrong.

My generosity was provincial.

His miserly spirit didn't get any better
with my friendly company, on that ship,
his lack of trust in himself grew worse
as if anyone were ever able to convince
those who never believed in themselves
to not wound themselves in their war
against their own shadow. They are as they were born.

No un enfermizo caso, ni la ausencia
de la grandeza, no,
nada puede matar nuestro mejor,
la bondad, sí señor, que padecemos:
bella es la flor del hombre, su conducta
y cada puerta es la bella verdad
y no la susurrante alevosía.

Siempre saqué de haber sido mejor,
mejor que yo, mejor de lo que fui,
la condecoración más taciturna:
recobrar aquel pétalo perdido
de mi melancolía hereditaria:
buscar una vez más la luz que canta
dentro de mí, la luz inapelable.

Never an illness, nor the absence
of grandeur, no,
nothing is able to kill the best in us,
that kindness, dear sir, we are afflicted with:
beautiful is the flower of man, his conduct
and every door opens on the beautiful truth
and never hides treacherous whispers.

I always gained something from making myself better,
better than I am, better than I was,
that most subtle citation:
to recover some lost petal
of the sadness I inherited:
to search once more for the light that sings
inside of me, the unwavering light.

Sí, camarada, es hora de jardín
y es hora de batalla, cada día
es sucesión de flor o sangre:
nuestro tiempo nos entregó amarrados
a regar los jazmines
o a desangrarnos en una calle oscura:
la virtud o el dolor se repartieron
en zonas frías, en mordientes brasas,
y no había otra cosa que elegir:
los caminos del cielo,
antes tan transitados por los santos,
están poblados por especialistas.

Ya desaparecieron los caballos.

Los héroes van vestidos de batracios,
los espejos viven vacíos
porque la fiesta es siempre en otra parte,
en donde ya no estamos invitados
y hay pelea en las puertas.

Por eso es éste el llamado penúltimo,
el décimo sincero
toque de mi campana:
al jardín, camarada, a la azucena,

Yes, comrade, it is the hour of the garden
and the hour of battle, each day
flows from flowers or blood:
our age committed us, bound
to water the jasmine
or to bleed to death in a dark street:
virtue or sadness scattered themselves
across cold zones, over biting embers
and there was no other choice:
the roads of the sky
once traveled mostly by saints
now swarm with experts.

The horses have already disappeared.

The heroes run around dressed like toads,
and the mirrors lead empty lives
because the party is always somewhere else,
somewhere where we are not invited
and there are fights in the doorways.

That is why it's almost the last call,
the sincere tenth
ringing of my bell:
to the garden, comrade, to the white lily,

al manzano, al clavel intransigente,
a la fragancia de los azahares,
y luego a los deberes de la guerra.

Delgada es nuestra patria
y en su desnudo filo de cuchillo
arde nuestra bandera delicada.

to the apple tree, to the stubborn carnation,
to the fragrance of orange blossoms,
and then to the duties of war.

Slender is our country
and on the naked edge of knives
her delicate flag burns.

———————

Desde que amaneció con cuántos hoy
se alimentó este día?
Luces letales, movimientos de oro,
centrífugas luciérnagas,
gotas de luna, pústulas, axioma,
todos los materiales superpuestos
del trascurso: dolores, existencias,
derechos y deberes:
nada es igual cuando desgasta el día
su claridad y crece
y luego debilita su poder.

Hora por hora con una cuchara
cae del cielo el ácido
y así es el hoy del día,
el día de hoy.

After sunrise how many things
are needed to sustain this day?
Lethal lights, golden rays crossing the land,
centrifugal glowworms,
drops of moon, blisters, axiom,
all material superimposed
upon time's passage: sadnesses, existences,
rights and responsibilities:
nothing is equal while the day eats away
at its clear light and grows
and then loses its power.

Hour after hour one spoonful
of acid falls from the sky,
as today falls from the day,
from the day of this day.

El puerto puerto de Valparaíso
mal vestido de tierra
me ha contado: no sabe navegar:
soporta la embestida,
vendaval, terremoto,
ola marina,
todas las fuerzas le pegan
en sus narices rotas.

Valparaíso, perro pobre
ladrando por los cerros,
le pegan los pies
de la tierra
y las manos del mar.
Puerto puerto que no puede salir
a su destino abierto en la distancia
y aúlla
solo
como un tren de invierno
hacia la soledad,
hacia el mar implacable.

Port, this port of Valparaíso
poorly dressed in earth
has spoken to me: it doesn't know how to sail away:
it withstands the assault,
hurricane, earthquake,
the ocean's wave,
all the elements strike
its fractured nose.

Valparaíso, wretched dog
barking in the hills,
they strike him: the feet
of the earth
and the hands of the sea.
Port, this port cannot set sail
for a distant unknown destination
and it howls
alone
like a winter train
toward solitude,
toward the implacable sea.

Todos me preguntaban cuándo parto,
cuándo me voy. Así parece
que uno hubiera sellado en silencio
un contrato terrible:
irse de cualquier modo a alguna parte
aunque no quiera irme a ningún lado.

Señores, no me voy,
yo soy de Iquique,
soy de las viñas negras de Parral,
del agua de Temuco,
de la tierra delgada,
soy y estoy.

Everybody was asking me when I leave,
when I am going to go. It seems
one of us had secretly sealed
a terrifying contract:
I must leave any way I can for somewhere else
though I don't want to go anywhere.

My friends, I am not going,
I am from Iquique,
I am from the black vines of Parral,
from the water of Temuco,
from the slender land,
I am and I am here.

LENTO

Don Rápido Rodríguez
no me conviene:
doña Luciérnaga Aguda
no es mi amor:
para andar con mis pasos amarillos
hay que vivir adentro
de las cosas espesas:
barro, madera, cuarzo,
metales,
construcciones de ladrillo:
hay que saber cerrar los ojos
en la luz,
abrirlos en la sombra,
esperar.

SLOW

Mr. Speedy Rodríguez
is not my companion:
Mrs. Glowworm Aguda
is not my sweet-voiced lover:
to walk in my yellow steps
one has to live inside
of dense matter:
mud, wood, quartz,
metal,
brick buildings:
one has to know how to close his eyes
in the sunlight,
to open them in the shade,
to wait.

SUCEDE

Golpearon a mi puerta el 6 de Agosto:
ahí no había nadie
y nadie entró, se sentó en una silla
y transcurrió conmigo, nadie.

Nunca me olvidaré de aquella ausencia
que entraba como Pedro por su casa
y me satisfacía con no ser:
con un vacío abierto a todo.

Nadie me interrogó sin decir nada
y contesté sin ver y sin hablar.

Qué entrevista espaciosa y especial!

IT HAPPENS

They knocked on my door on the sixth of August:
nobody was standing there
and nobody entered, sat down in a chair
and passed the time with me, nobody.

I will never forget that absence
that entered me like a man enters his own house
and I was satisfied with non-being:
an emptiness open to everything.

Nobody questioned me, saying nothing,
and I answered without seeing or speaking.

Such a spacious and specific interview!

RAMA

Una rama de aromo, de mimosa,
fragante sol del entumido invierno,
compré en la feria de Valparaíso
y seguí con aromo y con aroma
hasta Isla Negra.

Cruzábamos la niebla,
campos pelados, espinares duros,
tierras frías de Chile:
(bajo el cielo morado
la carretera muerta).

Sería amargo el mundo
en el viaje invernal, en el sinfín,
en el crepúsculo deshabitado,
si no me acompañara cada vez,
cada siempre,
la sencillez central
de una rama amarilla.

BRANCH

A branch of acacia, of mimosa,
fragrant sun of the numb winter,
I shopped at the Valparaíso fair
and with acacia and its sweet smell
went on to Isla Negra.

We crossed in the mist,
bare fields, thorny thickets,
cold lands of Chile:
(under the purple sky
the dead highway).

The world would grow bitter
on its winter journey, in endlessness,
in the uninhabited dusk,
if each time it didn't accompany me,
each and every,
the simple truth
of a yellow branch.

EL EMBAJADOR

Viví en un callejón donde llegaban
a orinar todo gato y todo perro
de Santiago de Chile.
Era en 1925.
Yo me encerraba con la poesía
transportado al Jardín de Albert Samain,
al suntuoso Henri de Regnier,
al abanico azul de Mallarmé.

Nada mejor contra la orina
de millares de perros suburbiales
que un cristal redomado
con pureza esencial, con luz y cielo:
la ventana de Francia, parques fríos
por donde las estatuas impecables
– era en 1925 –
se intercambiaban camisas de mármol,
patinadas, suavísimas al tacto
de numerosos siglos elegantes.

En aquel callejón yo fui feliz.

Más tarde, años después,
llegué de Embajador a los Jardines.

Ya los poetas se habían ido.

Y las estatuas no me conocían.

THE AMBASSADOR

I lived on an alley where every cat and dog
in Santiago, Chile
came to pee.
It was 1925.
I shut myself in with poetry
that carried me to the Garden of Albert Samain,
to the magnificent Henri de Regnier,
to Mallarmé's blue fan.

Nothing works better against the urine
of thousands of suburban dogs
than an imaginative crystal
with its pure essence, with light and sky:
the window of France, chilly parks
throughout which the impeccable statues
– it was 1925 –
were exchanging marble shirts,
their patinas smoothed by the touch
of many elegant centuries.

On that alley, I was happy.

Long after, years later,
I returned as Ambassador to the Gardens.

The poets already had left.

And the statues did not know me.

AQUI

Me vine aquí a contar las campanas
que viven en el mar,
que suenan en el mar,
dentro del mar.

Por eso vivo aquí.

HERE

—————

I came here to count the bells
that live upon the surface of the sea,
that sound over the sea,
within the sea.

So, here I live.

Si cada día cae
dentro de cada noche,
hay un pozo
donde la claridad está encerrada.

Hay que sentarse a la orilla
del pozo de la sombra
y pescar luz caída
con paciencia.

If each day falls
inside each night,
there exists a well
where clarity is imprisoned.

We need to sit on the rim
of the well of darkness
and fish for fallen light
with patience.

TODOS

Yo tal vez yo no seré, tal vez no pude,
no fui, no vi, no estoy:
qué es esto? Y en qué Junio, en qué madera
crecí hasta ahora, continué naciendo?

No crecí, no crecí, seguí muriendo?

Yo repetí en las puertas
el sonido del mar,
de las campanas:
yo pregunté por mí, con embeleso
(con ansiedad más tarde),
con cascabel, con agua,
con dulzura:
siempre llegaba tarde.
Ya estaba lejos mi anterioridad,
ya no me respondía yo a mí mismo,
me había ido muchas veces yo.

Y fui a la próxima casa,
a la próxima mujer,
a todas partes
a preguntar por mí, por ti, por todos:
y donde yo no estaba ya no estaban,
todo estaba vacío
porque sencillamente no era hoy,
era mañana.

EVERYBODY

I, perhaps I never will be, perhaps I was not able,
never was, never saw, don't exist:
what is all this? In which June, in what wood
did I grow until now, being born and born again?

I didn't grow, never grew, just went on dying?

In doorways, I repeated
the sound of the sea,
of the bells:
I asked for myself, with wonder,
(and later with trembling hands),
with little bells, with water,
with sweetness:
I was always arriving late.
I had traveled far from who I was,
I could not answer any questions about myself,
I had too often left who I am.

I went to the next house,
to the next woman,
I traveled everywhere
asking for myself, for you, for everybody:
and where I was not there was no one,
everywhere it was empty
because it wasn't today,
it was tomorrow.

Por qué buscar en vano
en cada puerta en que no existiremos
porque no hemos llegado todavía?

Así fue como supe
que yo era exactamente como tú
y como todo el mundo.

Why search in vain
in every door in which we will not exist
because we have not arrived yet?

That is how I found out
that I was exactly like you
and like everybody.

PEREZA

No trabajé en Domingo,
aunque nunca fui Dios.
Ni del Lunes al Sábado
porque soy criatura perezosa:
me contenté con mirar las calles
donde trabajaban llorando
picapedreros, magistrados, hombres
con herramientas o con ministerios.

Cerré todos mis ojos de una vez
para no cumplir con mis deberes:
ésa es la cosa
me susurraba a mí mismo
con todas mis gargantas,
y con todas mis manos
acaricié soñando
las piernas femeninas que pasaban volando.

Luego bebí vino tinto de Chile
durante veinte días y diez noches.
Bebí ese vino color amaranto
que nos palpita y que desaparece
en tu garganta como un pez fluvial.

Debo agregar a este testimonio
que más tarde dormí, dormí, dormí,
sin renegar de mi mala conducta
y sin remordimientos:

LAZINESS

I never worked on Sunday,
but I never claimed to be God.
I never worked Monday through Saturday,
because I happen to be one lazy creature:
I was satisfied to watch the streets
where everyone was working, weeping,
stonecutters, officials, people
with tools or with ministries.

Once and for all, I closed my eyes
so that I wouldn't face my debts:
that is the one thing
I kept whispering to myself
in all my throats,
and with all my hands
I caressed in my daydreams
women's legs as they hurried past.

Later I drank the red wine of Chile
for twenty days and ten nights.
I drank that crimson-colored wine
that beats inside us and disappears
in your throat like a fish in a stream.

I must add to this confession
that after this I slept, slept and slept,
without renouncing my evil ways
and without remorse:

dormí tan bien como si lloviera
interminablemente
sobre todas las islas
de este mundo
agujereando con agua celeste
la caja de los sueños.

I slept deeply, as if rain were falling
intermittently
over all the islands
of this world,
piercing with starry water
the chest of my dreams.

NOMBRES

Ay, Eduvigis, qué nombre tan bello
tienes, mujer de corazón azul:
es un nombre de reina
que poco a poco llegó a las cocinas
y no regresó a los palacios.

Eduvigis
está hecho de sílabas trenzadas
como racimos de ajos
que cuelgan de las vigas.

Si miramos tu nombre en la noche,
cuidado! resplandece
como una tiara desde la ceniza,
como una brasa verde
escondida en el tiempo.

NAMES

O, Eduvigis, you have such a beautiful
name, woman with a blue heart:
it is a name for a queen
who little by little entered the kitchens
and never went back to the palaces.

Eduvigis
is made of syllables twisted together
like braids of garlic
that hang from the rafters.

If our eyes follow your name in the night,
watch out! it glitters
like a tiara taken from the ash,
like a burning green ember
hidden in time.

ESPEREMOS

Hay otros días que no han llegado aún,
que están haciéndose
como el pan o las sillas o el producto
de las farmacias o de los talleres:
hay fábricas de días que vendrán:
existen artesanos del alma
que levantan y pesan y preparan
ciertos días amargos o preciosos
que de repente llegan a la puerta
para premiarnos con una naranja
o para asesinarnos de inmediato.

WE ARE WAITING

There are days that haven't arrived yet,
that are being made
like bread or chairs or a product
from the pharmacies or the woodshops:
there are factories of days to come:
they exist, craftsmen of the soul
who raise and weigh and prepare
certain bitter or beautiful days
that arrive suddenly at the door
to reward us with an orange
or to instantly murder us.

LAS ESTRELLAS

De allí, de allí, señaló el campanero:
y hacia ese lado vio la muchedumbre
lo de siempre, el nocturno azul de Chile,
una palpitación de estrellas pálidas.

Vinieron más, los que no habían visto
nunca hasta ahora lo que sostenía
el cielo cada día y cada noche,
y otros más, otros más, más sorprendidos,
y todos preguntaban, dónde, adónde?

Y el campanero, con grave paciencia,
indicaba la noche con estrellas,
la misma noche de todas las noches.

STARS

Over there, over there, the bell ringer pointed:
and in that direction the crowd beheld
the usual thing, the blue evening of Chile,
a pulsing of pale stars.

More people came, those who had never seen
never until now that which holds up
the sky every day and every night,
and more, many more, so many who were amazed,
and they all were asking, where, where?

And the bell ringer, with grave patience,
was pointing to the starry night,
a night the same as all other nights.

CIUDAD

Suburbios de ciudad con dientes negros
y paredes hambrientas
saciadas con harapos de papel:
la basura esparcida,
un hombre muerto
entre las moscas de invierno
y la inmundicia:
Santiago,
cabeza de mi patria
pegada a la gran cordillera,
a las naves de nieve,
triste herencia
de un siglo de señoras colifinas
y caballeros de barbita blanca,
suaves bastones, sombreros de plata,
guantes que protegían uñas de águila.

Santiago, la heredada,
sucia, sangrienta, escupida,
triste y asesinada
la heredamos
de los señores y su señorío.

Cómo lavar tu rostro,
ciudad, corazón nuestro,
hija maldita,
cómo
devolverte la piel, la primavera,
la fragancia,

CITY

Suburbs of the city with rotten teeth
and starving walls
bloated on tatters of posters:
the scattered rubbish,
a dead body
among winter flies
and the filth:
Santiago,
head of my country
fastened to a great mountain range,
to ships of snow,
sad legacy
of a century of fancy ladies
and gentlemen with white goatees,
polished walking sticks, silver hats,
gloves that shielded against the eagle's talons.

Santiago, inheritance,
filthy, bloody, spit on the sidewalks,
sorrowful and assassinated
we inherit it
from the lords and their estate.

How shall we wash your face,
city, our own heart,
wretched daughter,
how do we
restore your skin, your springtime,
your fragrance,

111

vivir contigo viva,
encenderte encendida,
cerrar los ojos y barrer tu muerte
hasta resucitarte y florecerte
y darte nuevas manos y ojos nuevos,
casas humanas, flores en la luz!

how may we live with the living you
or kindle your flame,
or close our eyes and sweep aside your death
until you are breathing again and blossoming
and how do we give you new hands and new eyes,
human houses, flowers in the light!

Se llama a una puerta de piedra
en la costa, en la arena,
con muchas manos de agua.
La roca no responde.

Nadie abrirá. Llamar es perder agua,
perder tiempo.
Se llama, sin embargo,
se golpea
todo el día y el año,
todo el siglo, los siglos.

Por fin algo pasó.
La piedra es otra.

Hay una curva suave como un seno,
hay un canal por donde pasa el agua,
la roca no es la misma y es la misma.
Allí donde era duro el arrecife
suave sube la ola por la puerta
terrestre.

It knocks at a door of stone
on the coast, on the sand,
with many hands of water.
The rock doesn't respond.

Nobody will open it. To knock is a waste of water,
a waste of time.
Still, it knocks,
it beats,
every day and every year,
every century of the centuries.

Finally something happened.
The stone is different.

Now it has a smooth curve like a breast,
it has a channel through which water flows,
the rock is not the same and is the same.
There, where the reef was most rugged,
the wave climbs smoothly over the door
of earth.

Perdón si por mis ojos no llegó
más claridad que la espuma marina,
perdón porque mi espacio
se extiende sin amparo
y no termina:
monótono es mi canto,
mi palabra es un pájaro sombrío,
fauna de piedra y mar, el desconsuelo
de un planeta invernal, incorruptible.
Perdón por esta sucesión del agua,
de la roca, la espuma, el desvarío
de la marea: así es mi soledad:
bruscos saltos de sal contra los muros
de mi secreto ser, de tal manera
que yo soy una parte
del invierno,
de la misma extensión que se repite
de campana en campana en tantas olas
y de un silencio como cabellera,
silencio de alga, canto sumergido.

Forgive me if my eyes see
no more clearly than sea foam,
please forgive that my form
grows outward without license
and never stops:
monotonous is my song,
my word is a shadow bird,
fauna of stone and sea, the grief
of a winter planet, incorruptible.
Forgive me this sequence of water,
of rock, of foam, of the tide's
delirium: this is my loneliness:
salt in sudden leaps against the walls
of my secret being, in such a way
that I am a part
of winter,
of the same flat expanse that repeats
from bell to bell, in wave after wave,
and from a silence like a woman's hair,
a silence of seaweed, a sunken song.

Sangrienta fue toda tierra del hombre.
Tiempo, edificaciones, rutas, lluvia,
borran las constelaciones del crimen,
lo cierto es que un planeta tan pequeño
fue mil veces cubierto por la sangre,
guerra o venganza, asechanza o batalla,
cayeron hombres, fueron devorados,
luego el olvido fue limpiando
cada metro cuadrado: alguna vez
un vago monumento mentiroso,
a veces una cláusula de bronce,
luego conversaciones, nacimientos,
municipalidades, y el olvido.
Qué artes tenemos para el exterminio
y qué ciencia para extirpar recuerdos!
Está florido lo que fue sangriento.
Prepararse, muchachos,
para otra vez matar, morir de nuevo,
y cubrir con flores la sangre.

The whole human earth was bleeding.
Time, buildings, routes, rain,
erase the constellation of the crime,
the fact is, this small planet
has been covered a thousand times by blood,
war or vengeance, ambush or battle,
people fell, they were devoured,
and later oblivion wiped clean
each square meter: sometimes
a vague, dishonest monument,
other times a clause in bronze,
and still later, conversations, births,
townships, and then oblivion.
What arts we have for extermination
and what science to obliterate memory!
What was bloody is covered with flowers.
Once more, young men, ready yourselves
for another chance to kill, to die again,
and to scatter flowers over the blood.

Trinó el zorzal, pájaro puro
de los campos de Chile:
llamaba, celebraba,
escribía en el viento.
Era temprano,
aquí, en invierno, en la costa.
Quedaba un arrebol celeste
como un delgado trozo de bandera
flotando sobre el mar.
Luego el color azul invadió el cielo
hasta que todo se llenó de azul,
porque ése es el deber de cada día,
el pan azul de cada día.

The thrush warbled, pure bird
from the fields of Chile:
it was calling, it was praising,
it was writing on the wind.
It arrived early,
here, in winter, on the coast.
A red glow lingered on the horizon
like a thin strip of flag
flying above the sea.
Later the color blue invaded the sky
until everything filled with blue,
because that is every day's task,
the blue bread of every day.

Ahí está el mar? Muy bien, que pase.
Dadme
la gran campana, la de raza verde.
No ésa no es, la otra, la que tiene
en la boca de bronce una ruptura,
y ahora, nada más, quiero estar solo
con el mar principal y la campana.
Quiero no hablar por una larga vez,
silencio, quiero aprender aún,
quiero saber si existo.

Is the sea there? Tell it to come in.
Bring me
the great bell, one of the green race.
Not that one, the other one, the one that has
a crack in its bronze mouth,
and now, nothing more, I want to be alone
with my essential sea and the bell.
I don't want to speak for a long time,
silence! I still want to learn,
I want to know if I exist.

FINAL

Matilde, años o días
dormidos, afiebrados,
aquí o allá,
clavando,
rompiendo el espinazo,
sangrando sangre verdadera,
despertando tal vez
o perdido, dormido:
camas clínicas, ventanas extranjeras,
vestidos blancos de las sigilosas,
la torpeza en los pies.

Luego estos viajes
y el mío mar de nuevo:
tu cabeza en la cabecera,
tus manos voladoras
en la luz, en mi luz,
sobre mi tierra.

Fue tan bello vivir
cuando vivías!

El mundo es más azul y más terrestre
de noche, cuando duermo
enorme, adentro de tus breves manos.

FINALE

Matilde, years or days
sleeping, feverish,
here or there,
gazing off,
twisting my spine,
bleeding true blood,
perhaps I awaken
or am lost, sleeping:
hospital beds, foreign windows,
white uniforms of the silent walkers,
the clumsiness of feet.

And then, these journeys
and my sea of renewal:
your head on the pillow,
your hands floating
in the light, in my light,
over my earth.

It was beautiful to live
when you lived!

The world is bluer and of the earth
at night, when I sleep
enormous, within your small hands.

William O'Daly has been translating Neruda's poetry for the last four-
teen years. He has published three other books of Neruda translations
with Copper Canyon Press, as well as a chapbook of his own poems,
The Whale in the Web. He currently works as Production Editor for the
Microsoft Corporation, and teaches as an adjunct faculty member at
Antioch University Seattle.